Growing Peas

Heather Hammonds

Peas are very good for us.
You can eat them hot
or eat them cold.

Peas are vegetables.

They grow inside pea pods.

Pea pods grow on pea plants.

You can grow some pea plants!

You will need:

a big plant pot

soil

pea seeds

a warm, sunny place

string

two sticks

water

Pea plants need soil
to help them grow.
Their roots go down into the soil.

Put some soil into the pot.

Pea plants like to climb up things.
They grow little shoots
to help them hold on.

Put the sticks into the pot.
Then put the string around the sticks.

Pea seeds look dry and brown, but they will grow when you plant them.

Put the pea seeds into the soil. Put them next to the string.

Peas need lots of sun
to help them grow.
They need water every day, too.

Put the pot in a warm, sunny place.
Give the pea seeds some water.

Pea seeds will grow

when they have soil, sun, and water.

Water your pea seeds every day.

They will start to grow under the soil.

A little root

comes out of the pea seed

when it starts to grow.

A little shoot

comes out of the pea seed, too.

Soon you will see some little pea shoots.

Pea plants grow and grow.

Flowers grow on big pea plants.

Take care of your pea plants.

They will climb up the string.

They will grow some flowers.

Pea flowers

turn into little pea pods!

Can you see the little pea pods?

There are little peas
inside the pea pods.
The pea pods and peas
will grow and grow.

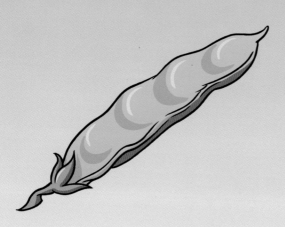

You can watch the pods
on your pea plants
get bigger.

When pea pods are this size,
they are ready to pick.
They will have big peas inside them.

Pick the pods when they are big.
Then you can eat the big green peas!

Leave some pea pods
on your pea plants.
Let them turn brown.
Take the pea seeds out of the pods.
Then you can grow more pea plants.